Consolation

Also by Lee Jenkins

Poetry
Persistence of Memory (1996)

Fiction
Right of Passage (2018)

Consolation

Poems

By

Lee Jenkins

International Psychoanalytic Books (IPBooks)
New York • http://www.IPBooks.net

Consolation

Published by IPBooks, Queens, NY
Online at: www.IPBooks.net

Copyright © 2021 Lee Jenkins

The following poems appeared earlier in another form in *Persistence of Memory* and are reprinted here: "We must Love our Friends," "Touching Under the Table," "His Bride is Black," and "Twoy Boy."

The long poem,"City on the Hudson," was featured in Frontier Poetry in 2019 (https://www.frontierpoetry.com/2019/10/25/poetry--lee-jenkins/).

ISBN: 978-1-949093-81-0

Contents

CONTENTS

What is the antidote to shame?

Part I

Are You Surprised?

Are you surprised
you wake up,
on cue, every morning

a little before the alarm
blares its music
and you lie there

a rousing, thoughtful clam
not knowing where
you'd been, unless

fragments return
of that journey,
a place you understand

but the men wore
their boneracks for clothing
or the children played

in pens fractiously happy
eating their ice cream
and BMs.

Though all of this
may shock
it's not surprising

like hereditary illness
in the family and the regimen
of its tenuous cure

or the body
in bed next to you
breathing so quietly

you had never seen her
till now—lying
facing you, her palms

under her cheeks as in prayer—
fearing to wake her
by your wondering stare.

The Intelligent Appearance of Things

*I*s beauty
more powerful
than intelligence?

The appearance of a thing
is first more real
than what it means
if meaning anything
is teasing out the thing
that struck your fancy,
an idea only as immense
as the starry sky
you're staring at

and the fine shape
of the eyes and brow
examined in a painting.

I am close to one
who thinks appearance
less vital than thought,

a striking blonde
can only be dumb
and the long catalogue

of petty heart throbs
an annoying diversion
from hard-earned

labors of the mind
like pi or Newton's laws.
I am still struck

by the perfect mesh
of hand and glove
or even the dexterous

posturing of a thing
whose motion shapes
an idea of loveliness.

Bird Feeding

Today I hung up the fourth bird feeder
with a squirrel-inhibiting weighted spring
designed for cardinals, chickadees and finches.

It's autumn now and the birds seem
more intensely feeding as they did in spring
arriving with the same light flightiness

and the sunlight filtering through their wings.
The hummingbird alighted at his post apart,
sipped his straw through the port holes,

beeped after a sip and was gone,
the buzz of his wings still lingering.
I think that if I strain hard enough

he will come again, because of my beckoning.
I think that if I stand long enough
the others will eat from my hands,

from obstructing facts bring forth
the dreamland, standing on the deck,
my arms outstretched like tree limbs.

The Invisible

*T*hat piece of steak
you're about to eat
snugly nestled on your plate
rendered microscopically
resolves into a crusty landscape
of rift valleys, eruptions
of interconnecting lagoons, lakes,
seething matter, bacteria, E. coli,
viruses looking for a place—
weirder and more real
than our dream-like parodies
or menacing giant ants in the movies,
compared to the really, unimaginably, unseen
nature regularly deals in,
a world beyond our sight
less we turn away in fright.

The invisible comes
in more mundane ways
like the wind, that
holds aloft the bees
or the subtle exhalations
of insects, trees;
and gravity, we are told,
that bends light rays

or holds in an embrace
when you fall down to Earth.
There's the power of thought
that lifts you off your seat
or lures to the peace
of the grave.

I remember a time
when I was a child
and saw someone close to me
converse with empty space
and ever since then
could never quite shake
the lure of the mind's second sight,
receptive to the idea
there's more to sight
than what is seen.

Camellias

I am standing in the garden
looking at the stalks of asparagus
that should have been

and the corn in its quadrant
by now waist high, as it appeared
for enticement in my dream.

I didn't even envision the cantaloupe
which put out much vine but spindly fruit
withered like the worms that fed on them

though the squash and pole beans
opened their leaves to the sun
and climbed their staves in oblongs

pendulously hung in yellow and green.
You donned a bonnet and sank
your fine knees in the mud

to harvest them for lunch.
Some of them we baked
in a steaming casserole with tomatoes and spice,

some we set off in a bowl
to be looked at, to grace the table
with our wealth from the earth

like the camellia we grow indoors
with its showy flowers, that press
upon us the sorrows of its siblings outside.

The camellia's bouquet is so subtle and sweet
the room seemed suffused with light
that colored the air with hues

of fuchsia and pink, of light
where there was none, as if air were sight,
and things imagined were real.

Angel Weed

Suppose you're weeding in the garden
savagely scouring, on hands and knees,

a righteous assassin of weeds
and all other suspects blithely flourishing,

crowding out and threatening
the visions of loveliness you planted

like boisterous school kids
cowering the timid, making you a little sad

having to shunt and uproot such vital insistence,
as along side the house

the yellow firelight of the wild
primrose shadows the strawberries—

and, weeding, you pause, noticing
a yellowish specimen altering to purple,

a dark-reddish sigh,
like the evening's drawing to a close.

Nevertheless you pulled it, it gave
and the afternoon seemed to pause

since an angel appeared, hushing
the moment with fingertip to lips

and put it back to earth again,
fading like wisteria on the wind.

Instinct

If "it's instinct for a woman
to know how to give birth,"

so it is for the thrusting of hips
the first time you coupled on earth

never having thought of what you'd do,
like opening your mouth

with a sober readiness
for ingesting of lunch.

No one teaches the mechanics
of loving, eating, defecating, unless angels

inform us in our sleep—
not the literal how-to-it

but the untutored doing of it
like a rose's unfurling.

And I noticed you didn't read in a book
the comforting balm of sleep, or scratching an itch,

on a loved face planting a kiss
never thinking in wonder at its strangeness

that one can feel at all
the wind brushing your face

or a noble attachment to someone, or a place,
that stirs the blood just by thinking of it,

as if somehow engaged, implicated, in the sunlight's
continuance and Earth's turning in space.

Touching Under the Table

Difficult to explain
the disjunction, between
the rude physical urge
and civilized reserve—

no slip of the tongue
to say she smiled on her husband,
maintained her friendly relations
got her life's work done

so that at her dinner parties
she'd place me near her chair
stick her foot into my pants' legs
and never once insinuate her stare.

We Must Love Our Friends

We must love our friends
in spite of themselves.
They bring a certain knowledge
we have taught them,
the comforting way we would be held.

Thus we learn to cherish,
grow old with them,
particular ones we have chosen—
out of gratitude and fears, honor and spite.
Emblems of ourselves, they know this,
gauge their own repute in our eyes.

In-Laws

There's the wife
of the brother of your wife
who thinks no one
sees her pretense

and your wife's
husband's sister,
who quit her job
to live an alternative life

selling spices,
making soap in tins
hoping for a hit
in specialty stores.

The first's
a preening queen
in the mansion
of her husband.

The other makes
a virtue of sacrifice,
defiant of her father—
a prince, who drank.

The cousins
sons and daughters
keep an obscure
recognition network,

fading orchids
of their loveliness as kids.
The wives are rooted things
in separate gardens,

the husbands glib attendants
with grins—and gins. Never with each other
do we talk about these things, except
at dinner parties with friends.

LEE JENKINS

The Way that the Day Speaks the Truth

The way that the day speaks the truth—
always nothing other than its hue.

The sky's a cloudy-blue, the wind's
a rushing through, not apologizing.

It envelops—outcroppings in the sea,
a hawk's generous view of the buffeting.

Is that rattling window pane
a knocking or embedded-thought game?

Looking into this, I'm reminded
of the day's glib surrenderings.

How deep is the what is not you, or me,
spoken with guileless sincerity,

appeasing half-truths, distracting,
locked into agreeableless space.

The boundless sky reminds
of the depth of withholding

as when knowingly you went
into the chill without a coat.

It Was as Strange

*I*t was as strange
as going to another country
and seeing a new thing

a commonplace creature
with snout and furry skin
not outlandish to them

but an intelligent friend
who congenially sat
as the table with humans.

Something as strange
as this and as routine
when I realized the absolute

conviction of my friend
to reject the pain of another
as contaminating weakness

lest he in his own marrow
experience it, not as a show
of sympathy but weepy

deficiency of strength,
a bleeding heart who cannot
stand what life dishes out to him.

Sure I'd seen something like this
but not the philosophical position
of keeping yourself intact

to avoid emotional comingling.
And, he said, resisting the other's diminishment
doesn't mean you're unfeeling.

Fear of Heights

*W*hat's involved in the urge
to jump, where you're looking
down from a spot higher up

not that you would do it
backing away from the edge,
yet looking feels lightheaded—

that you'd soar, before the plunge
onto the concrete, a garish splat
where the terraced planters

meet on the deck beneath.
To do it is release from all
entanglements, a freeing of psyche,

the price paid for dreaming
improbable realities
in the broad light of day.

Daring is precisely the blood
on the peonies, for which
there is no walking on air.

Is Happiness the Measure of Your Life?

Is happiness the measure
of your life? You are happy

the talk went well
your job is secure,

your date seemed pleased
when you called. It is good

that things go well.
A stroll in the afternoon

calms anxieties and fears.
But stories all end

with a falling out of love
as well as hapless falling in.

And the partner standing
next to you, a sympathetic ear,

tries and fails to comprehend.
What of your relations with friends?

A hardened character trait
defies your urge to rehabilitate.

Seeing the discord in their faces
is an ache from within

you know you'll carry to the end.
Does the happiest state

resist turning away
and record, instead,

the way we would shudder
telling real truth to the other?

The Mind Has Many Parts

The plane went into the building
so neatly done, you'd think
an antic performance artist
was riding the extreme of his luck
past even the lunacy of his own imagining.

It looked like a consummate work of art
and madness to say this,
but the eruption had a transfiguring beauty
like a mushroom cloud savaging the earth.

Perhaps you know what I mean
though having said this much is already
too much to mean, as we watch the ash
filtering down through the sunlight,
a shimmering flush.

Lighting a Fire

*A*mong the things I do
is light the fire in the clearing
under the tall oaks arching over
whose limbs are free of flame
though the heat seems searing.

A fire is a wonderful thing,
a cleansing, warmth and light producing,
an igniter of thoughts arcane.
I look behind for the line of flame
leaping to the can of gasoline in my hand

as if my intent were to see
how the flames ate up the ground
on the way back to the basement,
whether water through the garden hose
would douse the flaming house to sodden ash,

sort of akin to not thinking too hard
about something, less it happen,
the thought remaining a strange possibility,
though the light of this idea
easily dies with the flames in the clearing

now sinking down into night
and the crickets' din, an extinguishing chorus.
I turn from the window and sit again
at my desk, happy with the objects there,
the confirmation given of nothing really peculiar about my life.

Five a.m.

*A*t five a.m.
I jog along the Hudson
in a jaunt to clear my head—
or *walk,* in a duel
with arthritis—
feeling out of time
before the plunge
into the day's activities
like the tugboat, nosing
the freighter on the river
and spills from overturned cans,
the path ahead
leading to oblivion,
lines of cherry trees
a map of time's end.

What's the point of running?
One at home
pledges me to it,
to keep alive a pact,
the acceptance of our deaths,
accommodating to it,
organic cooking, yoga,
our strong belief in effort.

There's also sweaty exuberance
resurgent muscles equal to intent,
a pounding on the pavement
in a dash of second wind…

Everyday Transcendence

When your marriage failed
and your daughter didn't get into Harvard,
the memory of your 6th grade games
still fresh in your mind,
one of the last to be chosen—
what needed to be said never spoken—

when the arrow you selected
pierced the target,
in spite of the vagaries
of wind, slant of light
and distance from your hand—
did you will the inevitable
as your own, alive to the life
selected for you only?

A Means of Attachment

*I*f she could speak
he would listen, repeating
the gist of what he heard.
He'd retreat, no doubt,
from his position.
She'd rediscover passion,
hearing his holding
of her words.
But she speaks incessantly
of nothing at all
like the certain raising up
of a dike
to keep real hurt
out of sight.
It lies there wounded
in the field,
stalks they look at
wondering the source
of such blight.
He's learned how
to ply a balm
of kindness to them,
scared to disrupt the earth, forge
emergent new growth—
such is the burying
of their hope.

Me and Not Me

You were not looking at me
and I was still there.

Your not looking
made me see you

in all your
improbability,

like a child being held,
crying inconsolably

who cannot see, holding him,
the Mommy of his idea.

The beautiful things
you made oppressed me

with their loveliness
of yearning and fear.

I wanted to kill
to be as desirable,

your absence something imperishable
in my heart,

my aloneness
in every thing, apart.

Sethe

For Tony Morrison

When a mother kills a daughter
so she won't be enslaved
withdrawing her eyes from her eyes
as she plies a rusty blade

having herself recently escaped
from that place of living death
where body and soul are raped
and pressed, at others' behest,

into just clods of unworthiness—
could love, or a mother's right,
send her (and her brothers) to a place of rest
somewhere safe in the light

of benevolent redress—
or mere guilt-ridden awfulness?

LEE JENKINS

The Problem With Desire

The problem with desire
is its circumstantial fire.

The glint of your earrings
stirs the memory of your limbs.

You slowly removed them
smuggling a look at my abdomen

undoing the clasp of your under things.
Your look reflected mine

in the fashion you imagined
I was thinking of.

That glint was the sparkle
of investment in us

when our own natural zest
had long been suppressed

by midlife crisis, multiple kids,
egalitarian sharing of careers—

a muscular chest, thickening vesicles,
plying of portals, pinioning breasts,

visions of embarrassing come on,
can lead also to a turn off—

as when you think I know
you're watching porno.

Loving attachment is a partnering
exchange of similarities.

Ecstatic sex is a partnering
embracing of opposites,

the rogue vitality of your grin
arriving home from gym—

that moment of readiness,
my all investment in it.

You Know That I Think You're Beautiful

You know that I think you're beautiful
because you also think so, maybe it's a law
of appearance that whatever is beautiful is good.

Your face is a mode of expression
of what is valuable, since its contours
draw the eye to see

what in itself is worth seeing.
Nothing will stop our staring at the ocean,
the finesse of the way you fling

your scarf in the wind, your hand
like the flight of an animate thing.
How cannot the good be beautiful?

I withdraw my eyes, thinking you think
how enamored I am of you,
that the thing that empowers is your creation,

not the habitation of something benevolent
that arrived like a gift from beyond
seizing some particular thing to make itself known.

Bitching

*H*ere's the thing:
How far to go
to defend your position

when you think
the other has
traduced your reputation—

and negligently dismissed his own—
by failing to respond
to the calling into question

of his own integrity
when you laid
down the accusation

of his lack of adequacy
in comparison to your own.
You were defending your ground,

trying to pin him completely down
not just for the fact of it
but the sweet exercise of wit

that can't wreak enough carnage,
like an overstuffed infant
still yelling in its crib.

His defense was to rise
above the fray, contemplating it,
like a kid in the park

who looks askance
at another's move
to commandeer his bicycle

lest he descend
to a level of strife
out of sync with his life.

So the two of you contend
yet fail to ignite the contempt
flickering in the eyes

like lovers rehearsing
a script that one day might
forecast their final demise.

Women in Flip Flops

The flap against the sole
is sometimes prominent
a clapping announcement
or feminine acknowledgment
of the flesh—an artifact, perhaps,
inescapably there, like breasts.

Feet and a web
of painted toes,
clefts, the unseen, glimpsed,
Things that peep and flash
like jewels in a keepsake—
a kind of ambience,
toe-hold on everything unsaid.

Part II

Consolation

(After Franz Liszt's *Consolation No. # 3*)

*E*ven though—the need for recognition
propels me, as the strongest urge I know,
to be respected with a show of self-

investment as appropriate to me, I mean
status and the assurance of having money
without too noticeably revealing

being assailed by such fears—
I haven't suffered enough
to hate the life I live, only the discomfort

between the evidence of what is
and what you privately assert to yourself
in a delusion of the real, your life of fantasy.

Don't those who know you know the truth
of this, and smile appeasingly, the pact of friends?
They are so willfully affirming

even when hosting a subject of distress.
The hard core of hatred is not felt
in difference of opinion but spiritual bondage,

walls of it, the unassimilable way you and I
are not imagined in the same pattern of cloth.
We are not friends but enemies, in love

with our difference as the reason we exist.
And if I love intensely enough
I would lose myself in the mix, glad

to be annexed to the thing I have claimed
but failed to accept as my complement, the brother
whose resemblance I resent, the lover

whose embrace is a chilling release
from the propped up version of myself I present.
There's a generosity in the passage of time

like the effort involved in trying to live respectfully
when one didn't appreciate the degree of one's brokenness.
So I have wanted to go down on my knees

for the blessing of the sun,
on mornings when the light
seemed an invitation honorably to live.

How to express this simplest of urges,
a way to fulfill this conception of worthiness?

New York City Subway

I have left the doctor's office
where blood was drawn for next week's
yearly assessment, of the continued
evading of prostate cancer, in my 72nd year.

The place was filled with the infirm and elderly,
every specimen of humanity summoned
to a rendezvous here, agile in step
or paper-thin figures in wheelchairs.

Death seemed an agreement we could
live with, the end result of a beginning;
so the young husband led the young wife
so big to bursting with beginnings, that

a frail hand was quickest to reach out
and hold back the door for her entrance.
Outside, having arrived at the subway station,
another elevator took us to the nether regions.

I was reading poetry, a sensitive rendering
of multi-racial identity, fraught
with ambivalence, how to accept
the shame of the past and the privilege

accorded the melded, multi-ethnic image.
But no fullness of self is un-conflicted,
I thought, given conceptions of strength
and weakness, traditions of beauty and beast.

"Morning, everyone, I am homeless and hungry…"
the veteran announced, to the subway car's assemblage,
to a response as slight as the welcome
given a terrorist. A long pause, in exasperation:

"Jesus! What's the matter, people?"
The taint of a common failing seemed to hold us
as he exited. I climbed the stairs to the sunlight
where a blonde descended, in the pride of her life.

Grandma's Sick in the Hospital

For Dr. Phil

Grandma's sick in the hospital.
She say, Ya'll ain't touch me
Till my grandbaby arrive.

That be tomorrow, or today,
Depending what flight from LaGuardia
He gets straightaway.

The surgeon's smile curls to a frown.
The bowel-blocking tumor
Will have to be deboweled.

Malignant or benign, we'll tolerate
This momentary pause for now.
Meanwhile her spirits are high.

She can leave this life, tomorrow, today,
With 94 years of turmoil and grace.
For breakfast, she say, My juice

And my eggs, but not that kind
In a cardboard box, even
The chicken be surprised.

Her laugh's like a child's
Rolling round in the grass.
And then he arrives

A beard and dreadlocked strands,
A wide, flat brow recalling his Gran's
A lightly carried MBA

A 2nd-year place in Columbia Med.
She glances him over her spectacles—
A look he returns from 20 years ago,

A barefoot scholar on the floor.
You be somebody one day, she said,
Her eyes in enveloping gaze

As she stitched a blue patch
Inside grandpa's work pants—
She saw that he thought she would die.

She say, You my emissary,
Take care all my business.
This ain't the ending. It be

Just the beginning. He saw
That she saw that he feared
His own bending, from way

Back when, the only one alive
In whose eyes he saw his beginnings.
From one of eight daughters

And sons, he was the gift
At her door sorely given.
His hand in hers,

Arthritic grip's pressure—
The consoling eyes' lift
He saw from a distance.

Nobody's Fault

1

What of the child
struck in the head
by a playmate in the yard
and nobody knows
(except, momentarily unobserved,
the 2-year-olds involved)
whose brain tissues swell
effectively destroying cells.
The hysterical mother faults
the emergency room procedure
after, a week later,
the child has had her first
grand mal seizure.

2

You were one of three
of thirty-six, they said,
after having been winnowed
from telephone interviews, crisp resumes,
an all-expense-trip
to the office in Toledo.

The unremarkable backache
of the low-slung chair, the perfume

of the prim smiling inquisitor,
making you sick, dredging up
a fit of resentment, having
to work so hard
and the need into your handkerchief to spit;
her genuine solicitousness you're convinced
still seemed her own self-indulgence, that
raised in you a rage to resist—
the letter, a week later,
that all your hope so courteously dismissed—
your anger at the thought,
as you viewed the night before,
that your angst-ridden,
difficulty sleeping
was at fault.

3

The unexpected remedy—
since the 3 kids demanded full attention
all the live-long day,
her thinking her accumulating plumpness
was a sin of her own failing
to infuse the night sufficiently with a blessing,
since you were always so tired or hungry.
You two seemed like complementary dressers
keeping vigil in that space.

So the other woman came into view
through comingling of your schedules,
then the drinks and the dinners

till you seemed one more couple
just pursuing the usual routines couples do,
the rooms for hire at first leisurely passed by
until, a week later, you were seen—
the fault of being persuaded
there's not too much difference
between attachment and indulgence
of your desires.

4

When the racist
thinks the object of his fear
is worthy of contempt
since all those he knows also think this;
when the hand of the stereotype
doesn't fit the glove,
or, when it's in it,
reminds you of your own tortured diffidence
seeking to be friendly in a strained relationship;

when your love is an arrangement
to maintain your self-esteem,
at the other's expense, without
your too much thinking this—
until, a week later, your lover
faces you in the hallway
but first faults himself
for needing to ask from you
some distance, and space—
the stifling again of your understanding sentiment

by your own self-centeredness,
which says *you're* the one always dismissed.

       5

What about extreme improvisation
masquerading as routine?
That your father also
never had his father, having
him a fine abstraction, theoretically
believed in, nothing of a haven
for your ideas, or tears,
though rumor quickly visions
the 2 in 10 inhabiting your dreams, I mean
the super-gods in the zone,
driving the team on
or the hip-hop entrepreneurial update
on the likes of Malcolm X or Dr. King,
or the uncle with no degree
who supported all the kin, and
the dentist in the loft
over the street,
not to be identified with,
who nevertheless
on credit did your teeth.

The others, socio-economic successes,
referred to in academic text(es)
or themselves writing them, reporting
on all our left-behind friends
who smoke and drink and sex, and die

of diabetes and substance-induced heart aches
entrenched rounds of intermittent work,
something like this,
laboring crews and such,
anachronistic dignity of work—
if the generational slide into oblivion
still wasn't finished, was pending,
awaiting the life sentence
on absentee employment—

and the women, daughters
and their mothers
or else a fierce departure
into the world's putative promise
through stick-to-it academics, endurance-pride,
makeshift men and/or family life,
a familiar kind of bearing of loneliness,
visiting the sisters on the brink
somewhere back home hoarding food stamps
in the apartments with the kids,
waiting on the penitentiary men, a love
beaten down to desperation and sin—
and, a week later,
accompanying morning coffee,
a keen, maniacal dream recollection,
a gnawing on the remnant of something,
scanned like some seepage down a drain.

6

That there's no assurance
your children will succeed
no matter how intensely
you've loved them,
or sacrificed, to provide
the proper measure of well-being
consistent with your image pride,
catapulting them on up
where they need to be,
emblems of middle-class sufficiency
who always land good jobs.

Now the hard-driving effort,
achievement test performance,
is its own reward. A horde
of gladiators is sprinting
neck to neck down the track
toward the end gate
where all the laurels wait,
encircling triumphant-fewer heads
and the money-bags elite.
No remedy, other than
continuation of this mandate,
a sharpening of your edge
deepening the friction
of the parent/child dyad.

So the fruit of your divorce
is factored in,

your hopes less truncated
than the hardening rapport
with more than one of them.
You seemingly start to think
you're no different from the poor
with their weak performance ethic,
any hope of generosity
in the world extinguished.

Yet you see the others
looking like yourself
exact same baseball caps
but managers of unaccountable wealth
beyond what you imagine as cash,
some kind of algorithm, proliferating,
like the multi-stored view
of a Park Avenue complex
looking up the street to the clouds.
More money you can think
of what to do with, men
with appetites of little gods
past accumulating mansions and art,
money enough to buy all
of any kind of thing
even clergymen, and sure, politicians,
slush funds
like the budgets of nations.

Meanwhile, last week,
in my chair and pizza slice,

a new type arose
above the usual talking heads.
Speak, I said, and tell
me something new, unsaid.
I liked her rumpled suit,
the force of her brow,
the glimmer of grief
in her blue eyes.
She said something like,
We must wait out
these disturbing turns of events,
this ongoing state of affairs.
No one really knows
what to do about our plight.
All that we have is *ideas*.
Then she smiled.
I thought of the night
the house was on fire,
we ran out of doors
in our bed clothes
and watched the flaming thing
burn down.

So I clicked the remote
downed my drink
continued to sit
thinking of deductions
for my second job,
how to get over
like those criminals.

A Kind of Enslavement

Near my house in the country on a hill
the cows lie in the pasture in the sun
easeful as the day passing through its moods
from dawn's grayness to noon

and I could wish myself
as placid as they, as though thought
were sufficient only to ruminate
from noon to the evening meal.

Not to retire from strife
but to find a way to think about difficulties,
as if one were always the poorest
and most pitiable, standing alone

in a room among the smilingly privileged.
The other day I didn't reply to the discourtesy of
a clerk in a bicycle store too busy
to bother with the restoration of my 1960s Raleigh

who seemed to imagine my inability
to purchase a model of space-age alloys,
exquisite gearing.

Sometimes you can't think fast enough
to say the pithy thing, while other times
the withering blow sinks back into its moral murkiness

reluctant to strike the exposed face in its cockiness.
With the generous vindictiveness of imagination
I looked down from my hillside place one day
on slavery's masterful debacle

source of so much misery and waste,
as if God's emissary of redress,
slow but certain, at last had awakened
and, with my kind of quirkiness,

begun the arraigning—from the scruffiest
redneck farmers with their ragged slave allotments,
scratching a meager living from the Georgia clay
to the plantation masters with their thousands—

a swift backhand that breaks the jaw
of all of them, women and men, as an introduction
to cowering, that henceforth unless spoken to
never presume to speak again

after which the tough part begins,
the recalcitrant ones immediately changed, updated
to black women and men on welfare
in the inner city, pregnant, bitter, drunk,

ghettoized, strung out of heroin, remembering
their former state with only a change of pigment,
members of the klan on the spot incinerated
by lightning blasts in the act

of desecrating the Cross in their wretched name—
one could go on with this, a grievance as deep
as the need to restore self-respect in the forum of race,
a longing for equity, a tortured disbelief in its province.

Who has not felt, pressing the uniqueness of his case,
an idea of sameness taking shape, wedding him
to a common failing and strength, a lofty distinctiveness
inseparable from the vanity and shame of the race?

City on the Hudson

1. Awakening

*D*awn breaks like a spasm
across the room. My mind wheels
about face, flits over towers of Manhattan,
returned from its dream-freighted cavern.
She's silenced the ringing, quick-limbed.
I struggle awake, spurred by her morning
preparations: a glimpse out the window
as she clothes for the yoga and the jogging,
then the splat pizzicato of some feet
as a child leaps upon me in greeting.
Caught in an embrace, I forsake my sleep.
He jostles and jokes me to the shower.
Then, in short order, the dog barks their way back from jogging—
we descend on the day within an hour.

Something's incarnate at the breakfast table,
sustenance and set familiar faces,
permanence of place, a fervor that accentuates
our merging of the races.
As a matter of health, as her state indicates,
I refer to her ruddiness or pallor, her "whiteness"
is a something in the eyes of others.

My nut-brown's reflected in her eyes, sea green
contours of the way I would be seen,
a caressing and stilling of the mind.
In him we are subtly revealed:
a bronze glint on pearl,
a storm-cloud of curls—
he eats with his hands, our own little earl,
golden limbs raised in a blessing.

On the Upper West Side of Manhattan
there's an atmosphere of calm intermingling.
The spirited Hudson shimmers like a wide furrowed plain.
Riverside Park's a meadow by the sea
where the whole world comes to do its picnicking,
tracing a time-warp from Kenya to Peking.
It seems a kind of existential home
like—seen from outer space—planet Earth's blue dome,
a nurturing of multitudinous life forms.

We three've settled comfortably into place.
Good fortune and fulfillment on our jobs
sheathe the delicate foliage of our hope,
the heart-pang of won-over grandparents,
affronts that quell the vestiges of hope.
So the sunlight fills the room with morning light,
sunlight in our eyes, on our faces, that blinds,
fervent like an insight or the origin of life,
such beauty of such faces in a nexus that binds.

2. A Subway Ride

*U*naccountably intimate—
not the claiming for one's body
of one's own communal space,
the know-how of maneuvering into place
or the impress of some spirit in the flesh,
unwelcomed, unopposed, breath to breath…

but the inescapable imprint
of the closure of the self,
an agent rendered separate and distinct
conscious of a need for human links
conscious that one ends where *he* begins—
sealed off, like strangers in embrace.

3. At Work

"*T*he strident trains that speed the goaded mass"
disgorge me with a herd of kindred souls.
There's ample time to stroll my way to class,
a black, composed, who's forsaken overalls
in tie, briefcase and sport coat,
a look both grateful and smug.
Birmingham, and sit-ins, and even Malcolm X
seem rumors of the past, or bedrock,
shoring up return of the repressed:
the alms-grasping hands are mostly black.
The frightful insane and sprawling shapes
that we pass, cease to even shock.

We're productive and happy in our fortress.
Plato and Faulkner keep their sinecures,
arraign the dreaming pupils at their desks.
Harried mediators in androgynous slacks, we assure
the continuity of the past, insinuate a precedent
for present unrest, the hunger for knowledge
or the good life—hubris and sin and impoverishment.
The melting pot's an overflowing cauldron,
a collage, across the walls of college,
and smugness—and privilege—mix with poverty.

Yet all seem underprivileged, like actors
forced to improvise their parts, divested of sovereignty,
laced into the current cultural harness.
They angle for preferment, a shrewd horde of novices,
shadowed by futures of interest rates and mortgages—
the professors, possessors of doctorates,
humanists, empiricists, lovers of any kind of Lit. (and
legions of hard-working adjuncts)
learned attendants to icons of wisdom and artistry.

"Good morning," (or evening) I say,
greeted by a corps
of watchful faces, illumining
our station, linking our paths.
Here something can be made
of the racial morass, submerged hatreds,
unkempt allusions to class in class, upholding
a tradition of fairness and forbearance
and the lodging of the other in the head.

The professor's a black and a man
able to signify by nothing at all
the entrenched metaphor of a caste,
and women, blond or brown-skinned,
must confront, no different from the men,
the secret hidden portion of themselves in him.

We talk about essays and stories
elucidate comma splices, theses and poetry
with a fervor after work that surprises
for tired adults in evening classes.
There's trust in Shakespeare and the teacher they see,
antiquated faith in the bachelor's degree.

4. A Dinner Party

*O*n weekends or days after work,
evenings every three or four months
we dine with guests, attending the comforts
of wine and good talk, a thick roast of beef,
in a consecrated clutch of swelling egos
launching jaunty skiffs through the barrier reef
of heady conceit, displaced promptings of Eros.
We down our drinks like traders in gold.

Everyone feels more than blessed than most,
discussing disparities of the ideal self and appearance:
not to know one is not one's image,
a silk shirt covering up a blemish.

The women hold forth against the men
arguing the might of the feminine.
The men are subversive in quick, reasoned, face-saving feats.
The laughing aggregation makes a ruckus in its seat.
Eyes are gazing out of round-barreled pupils,
the irises ablaze, compressing the black holes,
strange in one's gaze, calm like the eyes of hurricanes,
recordings of the temper of the brain.

At the head of the table is a long-limbed
brown-skinned black man, image of the souls of black men,
historical update on the charred thing swaying in the dim
morning light and the haunting evocation of the spirituals.

He seems a man acquainted with extremes.
The soft leveling brown of his eyes and skin
are registerings, courtly insinuations,
of the room's egalitarian demands,
framed by the table's black and white book ends,
comforting seductions of a yearning
to bring the world's dissensions to an end.

The host makes comment on worthiness, ambition,
the sky must know us as it knows the trees,
so tenderly holds, the rooted outreaching branches
and endlessly betrays, like the scattering of leaves.
He reaches for the wine, moistening his lips.
The room sighs in concert as it sips—
and the two at table's ends
engage with eyes that glisten.

5. Day's End

One collects the dishes, one scrapes the plates,
puts away edibles and feeds
the other's washing in the sink
as the dishwasher whirls its accompaniment.
The evening's firmly knitted into place.
Like over-filled vessels
the gaze of each reflects the other's face.
Hands hint a mood of being held
whether or not the thought, that moment, was real.
She meets him, extending a limb,
perhaps an invitation or fulfillment all the same,
as the satiny darkness filters the blinds,
a space into which they alight
weaving their pattern by streetlight.

My White Wife

Not the blond, pastel-like
translucence filtering light,
or the questioning blue eyes
a signature of white—

no, an efficient, pretty brunette
showing off an imprint
of the grandmother's cheerfulness,
a melding, practicality and innocence

like a long-handed-down family implement.
I, an import to the West,
recognized it, trying to reinvent
remembrance of home. I mean,

a place, somewhere, with one
reviving the grace of my beginnings
in the memory of the thousand tests
comprising her upbringing,

how a good thing is
all that it seems, in
the individual eye of appearance
and everyday walls of resistance:

the white hand on black flesh
as if skin were a sacrament,
the staring, as of a solar eclipse
wonderingly taken in, the not

uncommon event of two people
in their meeting of wonderment.

LEE JENKINS

His Bride is Black

His bride is black
and he is white,
it seems,
to the right degree;
but marrying black
and being white
deny his pedigree,
worthy captains
of industry and bright
filigreed daughters,
brusque imprecations
for proximity
to colored.

Marrying her
he makes her white
takes blackness upon himself,
spites his parents
in his eyes,
assuages some his guilt.
He could not be himself
until he lived within the other
and felt the closeness
of her breath
and lingered on her body.

Clans

I was thinking of our
farthest back mothers and fathers
prehistoric ancestors five feet tall
preceding those artisans

sketching on Paleolithic cave walls—
when all were one color and religion
speaking a kinetic Ur-language
crouching in the gorge on the savannah

as the night sky convulsed with lightning
and volcanoes
gave their skins gray patinas.
It would have been familiar supplication

to their undreamt descendants,
the wealth of division they had spawned,
as the clearing sky arrived
and the worlds to be, as yet undifferentiated,

rose from the crevice with these ancient ones.
This multiplicity, blue eyes and brown skin,
the hegemony of Nairobi and London,
seems no more than the natural world's description

like the light shaping
the subtle shadings of leaves
as I lay on my back
looking at the light through the trees.

I was a happy member
of a fellowship then, not wanting
to blot out the difference
between oak and maple

believing only in the family of trees
and not their singularity
who stand as they are
like communities of peers.

A Benevolence

(For the Police Officer
And his Urban Antagonist)

*H*ow we lie in the pride
of our vulnerability
immune to our need

to be blessed, as the moon
shines a light of benevolence
on the heads of souls lying there.

The window frame seems to be glowing.
You feel your divided self—
splendid and sordid accompaniments—

like basic entanglements of Earth,
self-serving arguments
inseparable from birth:

Each kisses the wife good night;
Both ignite a resurgent fight.
Each recognizes the mutual stand-in

each for the other, against,
act out the roles prescribed,
locked in a duel of the eyes.

Both cast their plight as a fight
for a place in the good life, always
under threat from the other
and insufferable defense of the Others

whose respect is withdrawn
the more one confronts
perpetrated violence in its forms.
Each is exchanged in the other.

A blow to the face
is the price to be paid
for willful enactments of rage—

and terror in the groin, denial
of shame, such force to display,
this twinship of master and slave.

One wakes with a headache
surprised he's alive; the other
only dreams of deaths in life
seared through the gut by crimes—

those he performed, those to him performed,
one the most innocent perpetrator.
The smartest thing is never
to whine. So the one

(also the other) is moved
to assume responsibility
for intractable burdens of time.

Contempt keeps at bay
the sight of oneself as the other's prey;
an emerging view of one's failings

rises in the guise of the other's face,
a tortuous embrace, that rebukes
and despises the brother, lest one investigate

(generously displayed) the need
of oneself to rehabilitate,
upending one's lock on righteousness.

So perhaps it comes to this:
The whipper and whipped
enacting an ancient exhibit

when what was intended
was a way to contain the sway
of our basest of instincts,

where the haves and have-nots
perpetually exist, a social discontent
unexplainable, except

in warring-camp scenarios,
the strength of our own self-investments,
persistence of skin color differences.

The red and the blue are symbols of this
in the absence of which
who are you, without such division?

A sadowy self
in doubt and confusion
blows a spectral kiss to the wife.

Her face in dim light
seems the perfect image
of all worth preserving

in life, wherever else
in the world
(knowing your hatreds)

you least expected to find it.
How to manfully reclaim
the receding idea of some

thing in yourself
worth saving, hearing the truth
of her saying it,

this giving-in of men
to the power dynamic,
victims defamed, the others
so easily exonerated.

At the Crossroads

When the attendants
rudely pushed him
eying his flinching staff
he stood his ground, assessed them,
the rod strengthening his hands
to blast their brains
to the winds, him
in the carriage including.

They didn't plead
the right of passage,
assumed for a king,
or know
the secret fate of him within.
They viewed the right of way
a thing inviolate—
no pause, or need, to explain.
Some things must be accepted—
and also must be rejected.

Greeks and Trojans

The horse on the plain
is a magnificent gift of the sane
that seemed to forswear
the folly of pride and plunder

and the notion of honor
that spears a thousand times
the heart of the other
to ease a loss of face among friends.

A mistake to think an embracing occurred
of such letting go? Rather, a redeeming
of ego, to stand among ruins
if obligation requires a softening of mind.

So it begins. I am one of a tribe
of outcasts, perpetually ashamed,
inflamed, wondering to bribe
the conscience for power

to reverse the terms of exchange,
blinding all who look at me askance.

Part III

I Feel as if I Have Just Awakened

I feel as if I have just awakened
in my 71st year, never having really comprehended,
truly seen what's there.
The people in my building, for instance,
have passed down the years
like personages in newspaper clippings
I read about each morning, acquaintances
perused until the next day's edition.
We speak as courteously as we may
with no expectation of our differences
like the mirroring frames of our doorways
into which we disappear as we take up
our lives' enigmas, comfortably inside,
remarking terse exchanges on the wall's
other side, muffled in meaning, like
the routine greetings we extend outside.
It seems like our version of sleep walking.
People I pass on the street,
souls released from institutions
who stand in a haze of hoped-for absolution
or walk in slow dazes toward the new
imprisonments of their meeting place;
as well familiar faces of inhabitants,
a coming into being in the lobby
as I notice the commonality of their strangeness,

78

like beings, marooned, from some other place,
opening me up to all my unexplored space.
The bright lights of the elevator
evacuate into a familiar hallway.
This outward recognition is a segue
to speak about remembering what I'd lost
on the days when I came home
to sit in the dark with the lights on.

An Iron Railing

An iron railing appeared
in order to help us mount
the steps into our building.
We'd asked for it when 40 years
of youthfulness had passed
without our noticing.
Strange, the little difference
of appearance in our eyes,
seeing the same picture
passing down a generation.
Then a likely aged figure
seems to stumble on the stairs,
the extending of a helping
hand to this apparent visitor.
Then the turning of a face
and shock of the familiar.

On Life and Death: Having Read an Article in The New York Times

There's a pine box always
or air conditioned crypt,
measures to stay frozen stiff.
Devices attached to suicide vests,
and too much drink or sex;
the reliable cessation of breath
in our own or the hospital's bed,
the opening to final aloneness.
In your own house or village
perhaps the barbarians' descent.

At a party one night,
no one was dismissed or humiliated.
We viewed our loved reflections
in our eyes; and somebody said,
in that unexpected way
that truth like an afterthought emerges,
"I'm glad none of us is dead."
We laughed.

What's the evidence?
Emerging in the morning
still encased in your skin,
the one next to you in bed
affirming a sequence of events?
Others, at breakfast, in the subway,
at your desk—where you spend
the best part of yourself—
consent to the conspiracy you exist;
you agree in the thinking of this—
not a dream, specific and strange,
from which in the end you awake?

Fatty Arbuckle

(For Alice McDermott, author of
the novel, *Someone*)

*F*atty Arbuckle arrived
at the price of her mother's
having expired and would give again
all that she had, to ensure

Fatty her chance, plump, flaxen-haired—
less a choice than agreement pledged
like standing to bear witness, going
to work instead of lying home in bed.

I thought about this one morning
lying under covers with my wife.
What were the links that bind
like the familiar brushing of limbs?

Something we had made without knowing—
intended, but beyond our reckoning.
I wanted to give all I had
with no thought of having filled an obligation.

The Bumble Bee

A fat bumble bee
accompanied the forsythia and me

and maybe was hidden
in the bells of the jonquils.

It slept its journey, satiated,
away from that wooded place

as I stared down the highway
mindful of arrival and a suitable vase.

Later the next day
standing in the kitchen

I thought a menacing thought
had taken shape

in the form of a yellowish/black blob
of madness that hovered above my head

and streaked like an hallucination.
I thought to grab a cap

and scoop him like a whiffle ball.
It buzzed and danced

and flew behind the curtain.
I shook him loose,

scooped him, ran to the window,
loosed him to the 5th story winds—

a freedom only in my imagination,
since he's still hidden in the seams

where I must go to wrest
him free to save him,

envisioning next week a furry object
plopped down in the sink.

So when he buzzed furiously again
as if to melt the thickened air

of the windowpane with the heat
of his wings, I grabbed him,

not really fearful of a sting
but of closeness to something strange

and thrust him out the window
where he buzzed away

as fleetingly as the thought
I'd had of him, alone,

away from his companions,
a new world drawing him on.

Sarafina

I am waiting
for your appearance
and you do not come.

The day is lovely
at the sidewalk table
I chose out of the sun.

So I make my order
and glance in the book
I've brought, conveniently

under my arm, Stiglitz's
take on inequitable incomes
and the state of being undone.

You will see me
when you come. As usual,
I'm the only one,

though I'm beautiful
and looked at by blondes.
The waitress imagines

a fat Amex card.
And I am one
not always yoked

to my smart phone.
So no call is made
to later be informed

of your late
arriving presence
sitting at the bar—

that you walked in
and missed me and
thought I hadn't come

and left before long,
a salvaging of pride
in a storm.
Likewise, soon
I was sitting in the sun.
Here is a complicated run-down:

Mis-arrangements occur.
Life goes on,
resentments submerged

like umbrellas in a drawer.
So next week
we agree to reset

our friendship's come-on
pursuing semiotics
of a man and a woman,

the factors of trust,
the difference of color
historical views of the other,

the human equation
risking oneself
to connect with the other.

The Aroma Therapy Seemed Sweet

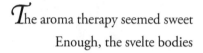

The aroma therapy seemed sweet
      Enough, the svelte bodies

Of privileged women spread
      Across the floor, engaging enough

To persuade that health and wealth
      And beauty were within your reach,

Prescribed by your sign, Pisces or Scorpio,
      Where you saw their fulfillment

Properly aligned, explored on a T.V. show.
      We were talking

With the cheerful wife of a friend
      Kneeling down as she painted

On a rock the flowing sails
      Symbolizing our resort, an expanse

Of breasts buoying her weightlessly up.
      I loved her for that bountifulness

That affirmed the goodness of life
    Like the luncheon on tables

In the back overlooking the lake, the grandparents'
    Grinning frailty in its wake.

A discussion we were having of the aptness
    Of whatever choice you make

If you think it leads to the lake,
    Proof being our walk on a rainy day

Yielding its portion of sunlight.
    It seemed a triumph of the right

Confirming a thing through its denial—
    Like a face rising to meet an un-proffered kiss.

Is All

Is this all, the jukebox voice
      sang out,

not so much a plaintive sound
      over the heads

Of the idling crowd, but the inquiry
      of a weariness,

questioning statement of battalions
      backed against the wall.

She thought a sweet jukebox could
      tell you all

the dragged-out thoughts you'd
      never spoken,

"Your eyes look cold"
      when you smile

and reach to hold me—
      a specialty

of involvement.
      Your eyes, knowing,

seemed to hold the world—
      that was all.

Living With a Narcissist

*L*iving with a narcissist
is punishment enough—
even the vegetables in the sink
exist as testament to her—or his--beneficence

in the paring and parsing there
into edible bits.
The dinner exists
with her—or his—loving consent.

I—we—try not to make
a virtue of complaint
holed up in our fortress—

living with a narcissist,
maybe, is what happens
when you—we—haven't loved enough.

Touching

Looking at you makes
me want to touch you,

as if to view you
were the same as entering

into you—your outer
and interior life

I would be exposed to, without
having acquired your permission.

This is why sight is acquisition,
holding onto with the eyes,

a way of touching,
just as any interesting thing

draws us into its life.
I am likewise exposed,

that part of me
in need of reparation

a way of completing something
being touched, seeing.

Love You to Death

Maybe to possess you to the fullest
I have to absorb all of you into myself

so that no part of you is left
to be what you are that opposes

or maintains its lonely island in the ocean.
That is what I want in myself,

an intactness that can rest on its shelf
without feeling deprived in its aloneness.

There is no end to this process.
So to love you is always a death sentence,

the finality of my need's an incompleteness
that feeds on the fact of your difference.

I Work All Day Sitting in a Chair

I work all day sitting in a chair
helping people recover the right
to consciously, more-or-less, chart a course
toward their deaths, without too much sacrifice

or self-regarding weight on their prospects or friends—or mates.
Some of us construe a way to make others guilty
of our own secret failings, seeing in their eyes
the imprint of surprise at something recognized and denied.

Without these complicities,
how could we get on with our lives?
And to recognize not the magnitude of suicide
but endless permutations of the need to be loved.

The gym is full, in specialty stores
you're ready to pay full price.
And Organic cooking, exercise,
will not prevent the tragedy of life—
though we try.

Looking at Buddha

I'm the shrink listening
>to the ruckus

her round face and wondering eyes
>question like a Madonna's

and pry and prick and pinion
>his mountain of self-serving facts.

On her part righteous indignation
>picking remains on a plate.

His the wounding contempt
>unaware of how he hates.

We surge and retreat
>tease out some reasonable truths

that stand up, stare, and sit down
>*Where were you that night I came back alone*

I myself would like to scream
>passing moments on the clock,

affirm the Good traduced
        both believe in,

speak of how the greatest hurt
        denies the truth of one's own dirt,

suggest the right to be oneself
        assures, sometimes, a torturing hell.

We've accomplished the probability
        of not parting

a steady tearless staring—
        and the bulge of her abdomen

emerges again
        a propped up little Buddha, observing.

Supervisor and Trainee

She comes because
I'm the supervisor,
she's the trainee,
a neophyte therapist
discussing professional alliance,
what she does with clients.
We look at instinctual urges
like sun-drenched lizards
strenuously inspected,
sometimes to be laughed at.
Her smile is pure as a child's
in the light of mother's,
mine like a father's
viewing the love of himself
in dependent others.
She has a way
of raising an arm
in emphasis, an incongruous
bestowing of blessing,
charming repetition
of someone she once loved
or still wished she could.
I want to cover her

with good wishes.
Didn't I say
she was beautiful?
Instead I remark her intelligence
as she crosses her long slender legs.
The measure of our passion
is the strenuous
posing of questions,
pleasure in discussion,
a thing wholly appropriate
that will keep preserved the ache
in the way she parts her lips.

LEE JENKINS

Would You Live Your Life Over Again?

As you and I were sitting
on the deck one evening,
I asked, satisfied with dinner, if
you would live your life over again

as a cooling wind lifted our gaze
toward the slightest flutter of the tops
of trees lining the river, pushing
autumn's haze into suggestion of winter.

You said that you wouldn't, would not
have ever been, and if no fact existed
of your ever having been, nothing *would* have been,
no memory of anything missed out on

except, you had to add, moments like this
as we eyed both the hummingbird and titmouse
flitting at their feeders, eying us and twitting
as your fingers graced my arm

though you feared to disturb them.
But this too would also not have been, I thought,
ready to live my plighted story again,
to alter it seemed almost a sin.

I wanted to be so important to you
that the stirring we felt, each thousand times we met,
was stronger than distress of all the present and the past.
It *was,* you said, but a deep irrevocability

can be still in the head, like the memory
one carries of all the let downs, failures,
stronger than hope when none was there
and all the crowning moments of happiness.

Can the Soul be Attached to a Place?

(For Yelena Kichina)

*M*y mother died alone in her house
after we had all left and gone away
into the conflicts of our lives,
her portrait of distress in our heads.

The neighbors found her lying across her bed
having conquered their fear and gone there,
since the lights had shone, a few days, all night
though she'd always been peculiar, strange to them,

fiercely inhabiting the solitude of her ways
seeming oblivious to their gaze.
I think she expected to wake up in heaven
with only the comforter slightly awry

from the rousing zing of her flight there
never imagining being dispatched
by a stroke's dousing the lights—
the way the others, weaklings, went.

Disparaging of both doctors and home remedies
she kept herself well through the strength of her will
since God himself approved of self-sufficiency;
and she painted, repaired, remodeled her house,

giving drapes their seasonal change and cleaning
and doubtless knew, after we had sold it,
the effect the owners' neglect had wrought upon it.
After the funeral, my wife and I heard

her footsteps down the hall, pausing,
as our feisty little poodle went out, barked,
and came back cowering between our legs.
It couldn't house her spirit now,

she wouldn't want to be there
so now I think she travels the air
and comes to visit where we are
and, in our aloneness, hovers near.

Closing of the Horizon

*F*irst, the lost word
and unformed thought
like walking in the woods

vaguely lost, the outline
of a familiar route ahead,
around the bend

no evidence
of the expected exit path.
Things seem to recede

as in a dream
like the retrieving
of the concept, *mindfulness,*

a triumph of the morning's
short-lived clarity of mind.
The reached-for cup

is no longer in your hand
nor is there certainty
the other car's not there

when you change lanes.
Not only a speed of 70
is problematic, unless

you're completely rested.
These are not infirmities
requiring special treatment

but the augmenting realities
of time. When you use
an aid, she can still

be penetrated, the urge
to kiss undiminished,
her ampleness a statement

of the prominence of your lives.
So a kind of letting go
is indicated. Little

can be missed beyond
the grasp of what you know
already is.

New York Botanical Garden

Because, when you took the car
up to the botanical garden
on the highway that's a fly way
on which everyone's revving for flight,

the faces next to yours in their canopies
cruising in lanes that seem to be heading
to a destination waiting at the end of time,
at which point I look across at you

and see the claustrophobic weightlessness set in,
fear of being closed up, swirling, anxiety's extreme—
it's time already to arrive at the welcoming center
so I raise the nose up over the Henry Hudson,

soar over Riverdale's middle-class enclave
gaining altitude for a right onto Mosholu Parkway
through the Bronx to Southern Boulevard
to our landing place behind idling cars.

What draws us to this place?
A remembrance of a need for solace,
something stirring that invites
a surge against everyday life's traffic?

As if the sight of roses, azaleas
sloping a hillside, were a category of things
conjured into being, to satisfy those cravings
for which there is no name?

A gathering of all the souls of the dead
granted a moment of song,
extravagant transports, a fluttering
of the air, an atmosphere that disarms

loosening proprietary bonds,
a rioting of peonies routing recalcitrant hearts?
Your eyes meet and hands make
a tighter complete, is the end of it,

walking back with an elf's sprightliness,
her face a fairy's, as you imagined this,
the mundane already calling,
putting the car into gear.

LEE JENKINS

Looking at the Palisades

What are those structures
nestled in the hillsides
fronting the Hudson
along the Jersey shore?

Emerging out the cliffs
they seem less erected
than eruptions of Earth,
terraced apartments

gouged out of rock face
recalling cliff dwellings
on mesas in New Mexico.
They glisten in the sunlight

as they might
to an explorer's eye
sailing up the Hudson,
at last quitting the ocean,

loin-clothed inhabitants, imagined,
or bleached bones of ancients.
I think of their crumbling
down the hillside to the sea,

not as a fantasy
or surge of tsunami,
but slow-grind impermanence
like the silence in a canyon,

cliffs driven up from the seabed.
Not every morning I think this
walking along the Hudson.
Sometimes they resolve into light,

pictures in a gallery,
from the mist of mind and sea—
something to be looked at,
that had not been imagined.

Was There More Gain Than Loss?

I noticed the stiffening
of their bodies, the levity
of their talking about fact-filled
declines of our friends.
I saw then the weathering—
she too sat among them—
of her face and hair,
a glistening of an idea
of the weight of the loveliness
of the past which stands,
altering the touch
of faltering hands.
Was there more gain than loss
of the day's steadfastness, say,
the 30-years' payoff of the mortgage
endless travail at the office
in an equal quotient of bliss,
like a scene of a painting
you've come to understand?
To be plain: has the measuring
of the output justified the means?
My hope each new morning
defends against yesterday's accusations,
a mirror of remembrance
I shave in each day.

Driving Home

Driving home to the suburbs—
last refuge of the earthbound—
grass and shrubs (I have to water)
and a nice view across the bay
that I left this morning, shrouded
in haze, as she left in the van
with the kids and the $20,000 tuition
for the mortgage barely saved, a lovely
ethnic transitioning place, where
a white guy—without having too hard
to think about it—really gets to know himself.
At the office we've orchestrated how to be gracious
when there's really no need for it.
I had a dream once
that I gave birth and
my father killed it. My shrink
made me think about this, a dream
of the price paid for always
having to do the right thing. But
what is it? I'm in harness
up to here for them. They're mine
and still the most beautiful. They'll
be back home when I get there.

She'll kiss me like you would
a lovely rose in the hedge
before you clip it, and tonight I'll
think of how to remind her
I am one who bears a spear.

Sex

I like the sex of your pose
reading the paper in the morning, an offering
of yourself to the air, lips pursed,
an unguarded amplitude of breasts.
There's a heaving in my chest
different from the in-bed joining
(an immensity quickly bridged)
against the further dissolution
of falling back again into ourselves.
At the breakfast table, you
have given me all that you have,
without knowing, an iteration
of that unthinking formal pledge we made,
I am yours to have.

We Walked Across the Lake Today

We walked across the lake today,
a trek, into a crunch, snowbound space,
noting the footsteps of preceding snowmen
waiting for a crack! then a plunge within.

New to this, we stood in its midst
imagining every streak of ice a stricken
slice of fright, like the broken through deer
I'd dreamed about, unable to climb out.

Did we yearn for the press of nerves
that leads to the extreme, as in
last summer's white water rapids'
headlong splashing down a rock-strewn stream?

Here was no life jacket, only assurances
these opaque window panes weren't going to break.
You could drive in your Camry on 5 inches thick.
Onward we went. Our house came into view

about midpoint the lake, the cleared
ice-skating space, marred with streaks,
adjacent the harbor, the stepping onto ground
having walked on water.

The Heron

*T*hen something came in for a landing
from some ultimate habitation
that could not be imagined.
I saw the equation of a thing

stretched-out in flight, suddenly arrested,
a buffeting of wings, and mass, descending,
the exclamation of a pirouette
of legs, extending, sinking into sand.

Why not a god's visitation
stripped down to essentials, chosen
for the revelry of this particular thing.
Certainly its step by step delay

and slow advance was a magisterial
mastery of the management of time,
since a quick jab brought up
a wiggly glob of protoplasm,

a devouring globbledegook
down the S of the neck's crook
and depositing *thunk,* I thought,
satisfying as the sniffed bouquet

116

of a glass of chardonnay
into a pair of hovering nostrils.
I watched from the deck
wanting to preserve that part

of me in awe of the bird,
the vague uneasiness that accepts
the cycle of triumph and loss
and their complementariness.

Max, Also Known as Puppy

Having completely lost his sight
does not stop the dogged
blundering onward toward the light
of the food bowl, or tough

posturing outside at the fireplug.
Odors still are sweet
as blind rebukes of other dogs.
We meet the 5:30 a.m. call to the street

or else a puddle on the floor.
Something aged, unique, or simply powers
of the Yorkie—one flight up
falling off the deck into the flowers

without breaking his neck—
standing, a dazed, What the heck!

Natasha, Also Known as Missy

I think she does love me
but she will not say. Instead,
she comes to dawdle and be
regal, circling me, in order to lay

her supple body down
richly secreted in a pile
and eye me upside down
as if to dare the thought

of something both domestic and wild
that binds the agreement we wrought—
engendering my smile—
as she winks, and retracts her claws.

Her point made, she leaves with a stare
like the view down the darkened basement stair.

Twoy Boy

He pants, after our run,
like an overheated engine
his lathered, gasping form
he plants in front of the fan

eyeing me with mild almond eyes
at an angle, suggesting
a benign Egyptian god's,
his coat slick, ready still to run.

There's a spiky red interior
with rubbery jowl-like ridges
like a jagged pair of scissors
or a grinning dinosaur.

After all-night howling
and a rainstorm,
we found him, un-weaned,
in the woods—rat-tailed

a flea-bitten handful
who scampered to my son.
The farmer and his dam
were knee-deep in a rangy

surge of mouths. So we took
our pug-nosed gift from the forest,
that summer, when aging parents
beat back their misgivings

striving for the lucky second sibling,
attentive to the body, urging
its compliance through a fervid mix
of will and rude biology.

Conscious of his function,
he barks forth his favor, willful
and shrewd, very likely human
fearful still of owls and the dark.

Suppose the Brain is not the Maker of Consciousness

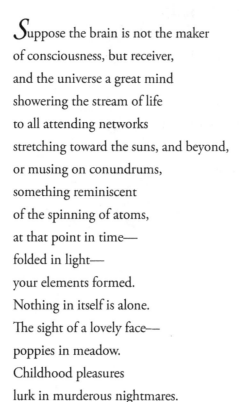

Suppose the brain is not the maker
of consciousness, but receiver,
and the universe a great mind
showering the stream of life
to all attending networks
stretching toward the suns, and beyond,
or musing on conundrums,
something reminiscent
of the spinning of atoms,
at that point in time—
folded in light—
your elements formed.
Nothing in itself is alone.
The sight of a lovely face—
poppies in meadow.
Childhood pleasures
lurk in murderous nightmares.
Each day
brings profusion
of interesting news,
a privilege we can

scarcely hold onto.
I made my way
to the end of my day,
thankful and obtuse
but imagining a benefit,
to make something
of this moment, as though
it were the messenger
of an unfathomable truth.

Tugboats and Freighters

*W*hy do tugboats and freighters
just sit in the river, sometimes,
the buildings at water's edge
observing monoliths?

I know the two gulls
perched on the pilings, ageless;
and the course of the river
from the shore keeps its distance.

These things seem signatures
of the world's sufficiency, overlooked,
like the slowly furrowing face—I
noted it—of one I love.

Images seem the essence of things:
departing faces glimpsed through windows,
what passes for the dead in hospice beds,
startling enactments on the street outside.

I carry a portrait in my head
of one who held me in her gaze
asking about Emerson's "Self-Reliance"
I had read, a potent, diminutive figure

standing in front on the class, as I sat
among school friends at my desk,
her encouraging smile an armor I could wear,
her arms folded bastions across her breasts.

Geese Over the Hudson

One thing I know:
they sailed over me
like the suave bottom
of a boat, cruising the air
over seabed,
feet tucked under them
necks taut, like peals of a bell;
a humming sound—
organotronics, I said,
a plunging of wings
and organ systems in air.
I wanted to scream
down the rapture
of the morning, walking
along the Hudson.
Maybe, trudging back up
through the gardens,
weighing the massive
granite of the stair,
to Broadway, I'd carry
still a gleam of remembering
like the honk of the geese
disappearing, back into air.

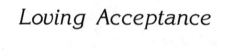

Loving Acceptance